A Day in the Life of a Roman Charioteer

written by Scoular Anderson

illustrated by David Shenton

Severus, the charioteer

My name is Severus. I'm sixteen,
I'm a charioteer and I'm very happy.
Why? I've just won my first chariot race!

I'm a slave and I used to work as a **groom** in the Greens' stable. That's where I learned how to handle horses. Then one day the Blues' stable bought me and trained me as a charioteer.

Getting ready for the race

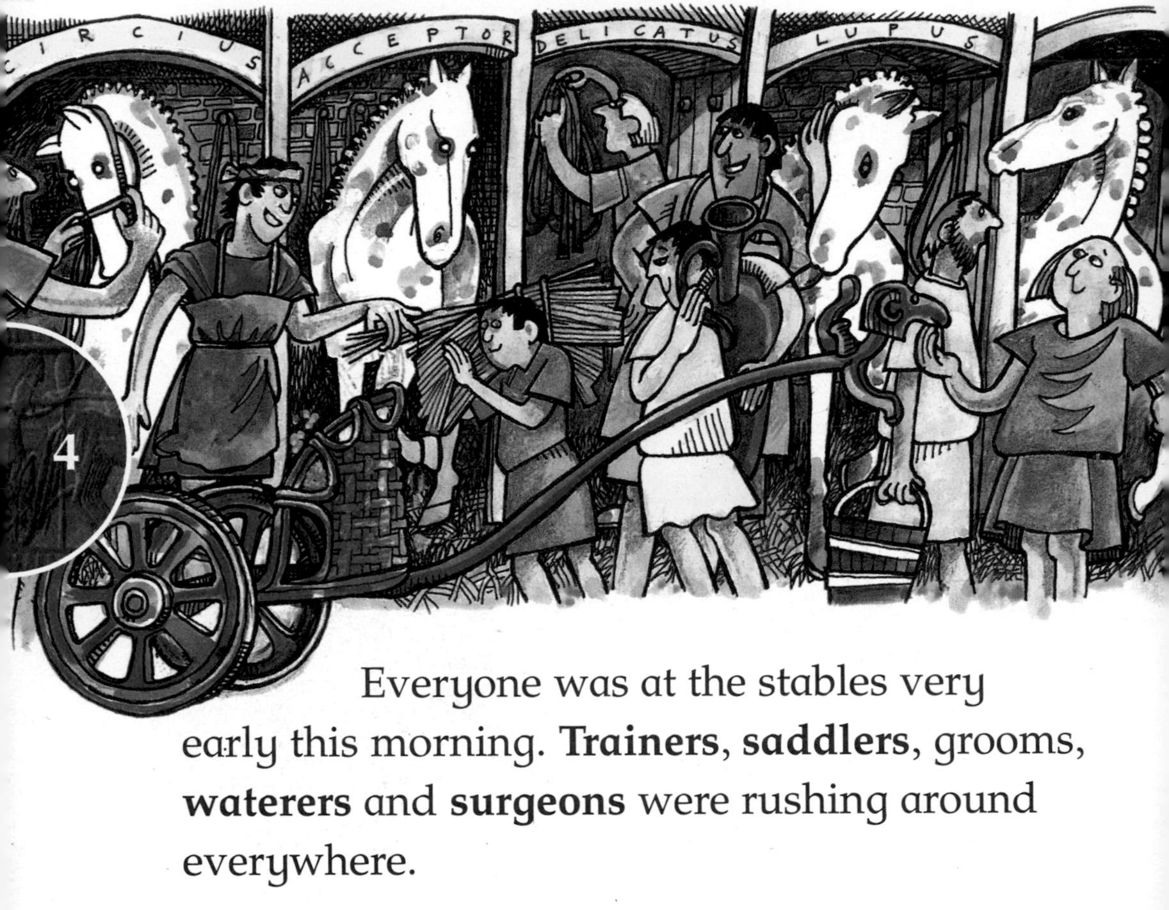

Everyone was at the stables very early this morning. **Trainers**, **saddlers**, grooms, **waterers** and **surgeons** were rushing around everywhere.

Even the club owner was there. He's a wealthy businessman. He owns the stables, the horses and the charioteers.

I inspected my chariot. A racing chariot is light. It's made of wood and **wickerwork**. I'm small and light, too, so I make a good charioteer.

Then I went to see my horses. I was given four of the best horses to race with. They were called Circius, Acceptor, Delicatus and Lupus. If racing horses win lots of races they can become very famous. So can the charioteers.

Then I put on my racing clothes.

A helmet

A blue tunic – blue is our club colour

A leather waistcoat on top

Long trousers with protective patches sewn into them

I went to the little **shrine** in the stable-yard and prayed to Castor, the god of **horsemanship**, to give me luck in the race.

Some charioteers write a **curse** to put on their rivals. They believe the gods will read the curse, and hurt their rivals.

I call upon you, o demon, from this moment, to kill the horses of the Green and White clubs and crush completely the drivers Clarus, Felix and Romanus, and that you leave not a breath in their bodies.

The sort of curse that a charioteer might put on his rivals

The fans arrive

I could see the fans passing outside the stables. The whole city seemed to be going to the races! They were wearing their club colours and chanting. There are four clubs in the city: the Greens, the Blues, the Reds and the Whites. There were soldiers in the streets to stop any trouble.

The **circus**, where the races take place, is down the street from the stables. People were buying things from the shops at the entrance. Some people bought programmes. Some people bought food and drink. Many bought cushions to sit on. The races go on all day, so they wanted to be comfortable.

Shopkeeper selling food

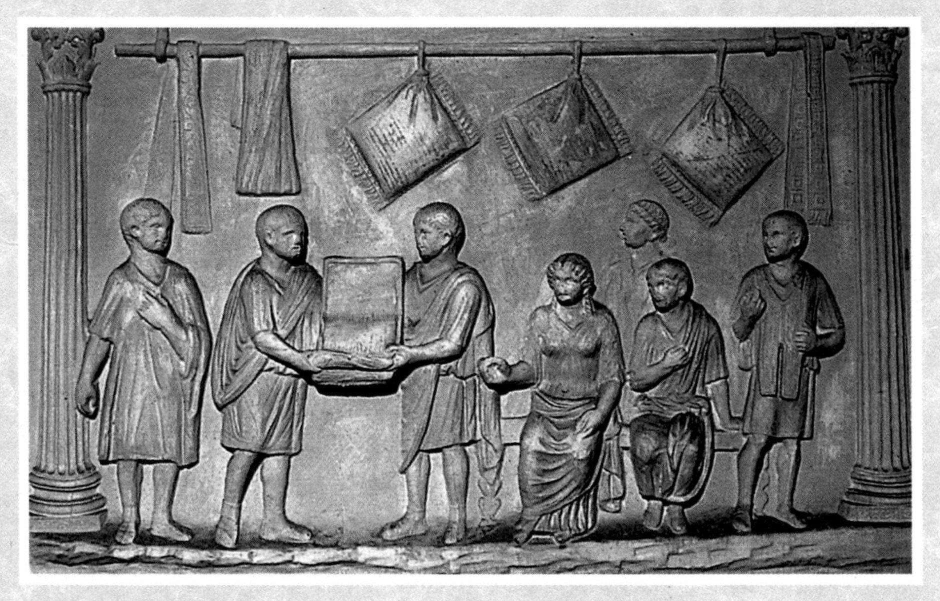

Roman sculpture of a shop selling cushions

People bought souvenirs too. Things like portraits of famous charioteers, and pots and dishes with the names of their favourite horses on them.

Mosaic of two famous horses

At the gates of the circus people handed over their tokens so that they could get in. Then they rushed to find the best seats.

This is a model of Ancient Rome

All sorts of people go to the races. The rich people sit on stone benches. They are nearest to the track. If you don't have much money you stand at the back. It's a great place to meet people.

Procession to the race track

When the circus was full of people it was time to begin. The race starts with a big procession to the circus. All the clubs form a long line. The charioteers ride in their chariots. The horses wear ribbons in club colours. They have lucky charms round their necks and their tails are tied in fancy knots. The back-up teams march behind. Then come the musicians, dancers and acrobats.

The priests come last. They carry statues of the gods, because the races are held to honour the gods.

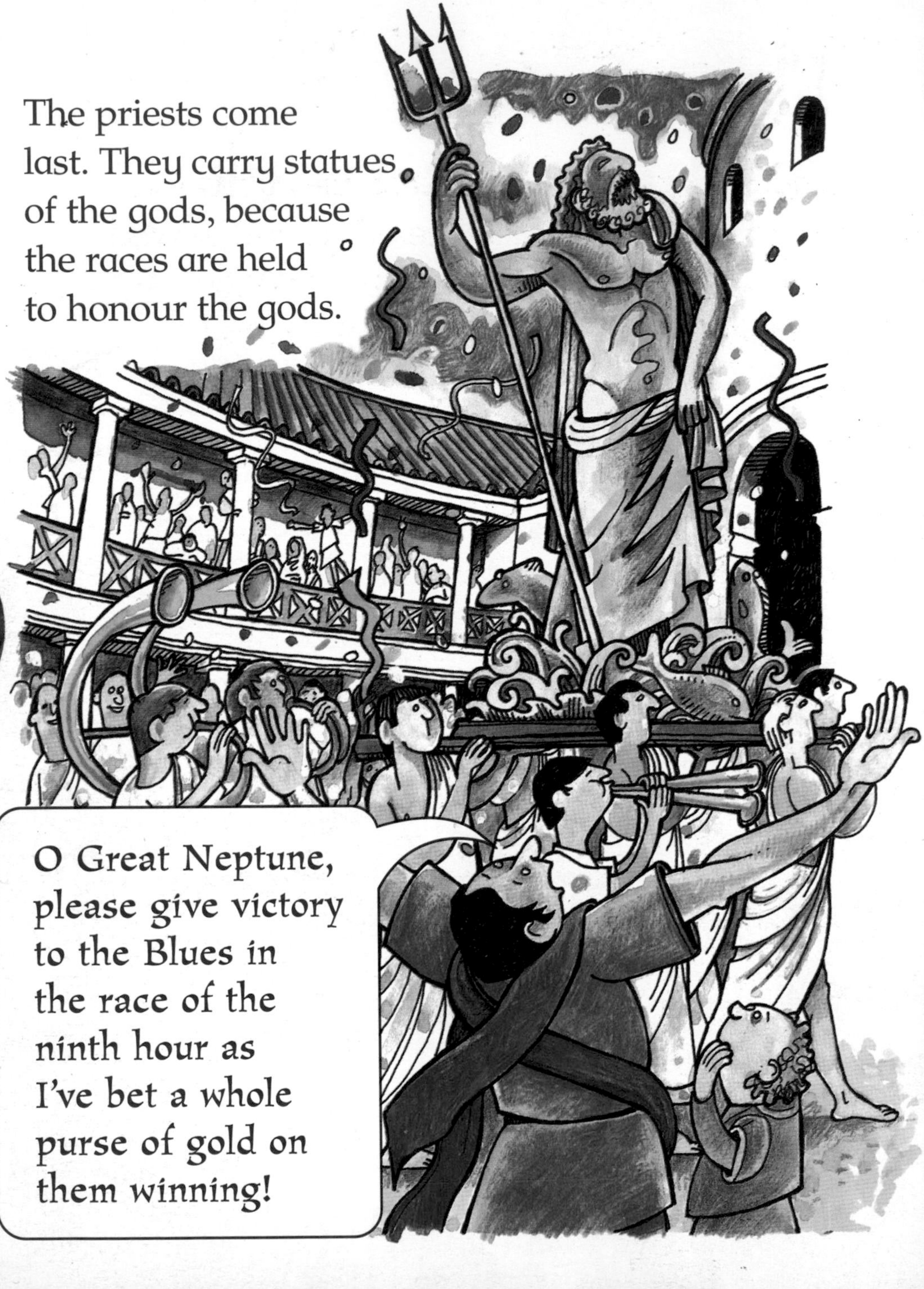

O Great Neptune, please give victory to the Blues in the race of the ninth hour as I've bet a whole purse of gold on them winning!

The circus

When the procession entered the circus the crowd roared. People cheered us and waved club banners. There were about 200 000 people in the circus. Imagine the noise! I was very proud to be there.

The race track is 600 metres long from the entrance to the starting boxes. I was in the first race with the other junior charioteers. Each club had two chariots in the race.

We drew lots to find out which starting box we would go into. I drew a box close to the inside of the track which was good.

The chariots have to race down one side of the circus, make a sharp turn, then race back. The race is seven laps of the track. In the middle of the track is an island called the **spina**. On the spina there is a rack holding seven bronze dolphins, one for each lap. A dolphin is taken off the rack after every lap.

The race

A Roman charioteer's whip

I backed my chariot into the starting box and the gates were closed. My groom tried to calm the horses. They were eager to be off, and so was I. I tied the reins round my waist so that my hands were free. My whip was in one hand. I put my knife in my belt. The knife is in case we crash. I use it to cut the reins free from my waist so that I can leap free.

I was ready.

The Emperor, who had paid for these races, stepped into the royal box. He wore a crown of gold leaves on his head and held an ivory **baton** in one hand. In his other hand, he held a white scarf. He drops the scarf to begin the race. The crowd cheered.

Suddenly the scarf dropped and the starting gates flew open. The chariots rushed forwards. I kept to my own marked lane for the first few hundred metres. Then I tried to get into a good position. I tried to get as near to the front as I could. Ahead of me lay seven laps and thirteen dangerous turns.

Round and round we went. The track was made of sand, and you can imagine how that sand filled the air as we raced! The club managers shouted instructions. Young boys ran between the chariots with buckets of water to wet the sand. One by one the dolphins on the spina came down. I was in fourth place. My team-mate was behind me. There were two laps to go.

A chariot race

Ahead of me, a charioteer for the Reds pulled out of the race. His horses were tired out. I passed a Greens' chariot at the next turn. He took the corner too wide and I passed him on the inside. That left only a Whites' chariot between me and victory. At the last turn the Whites' charioteer lost control. His horses stumbled and fell. His chariot was smashed to bits.

I had won my first race! I did a lap of honour round the circus.

I was given the winner's palm-branch and a purse of gold. My name was written up on the scoreboard along with the winners of other races.

A charioteer's life

I want to be a miliario – a star charioteer who has won over a thousand races. I will be rich and famous and I will buy my freedom from slavery.

Racing is dangerous, though. A charioteer's life can be short. A grave stone near the circus reminds me of this.

Here lies Marcus Tatianus, pride of the noisy circus, short lived. A slave by birth who lived twenty years, eight months and seven days.

He won 125 palms.

Glossary

baton a short stick, sometimes used as a sign of importance

circus a round or oval stadium, lined with seats in rows, where races and other entertainments take place

curse words said to wish destruction or misery on another person

groom someone who cares for horses

horsemanship the skill of riding a horse

saddler a person who looks after the saddles, reins and other racing equipment

shrine a place for worshipping a god, a very small church or temple

spina the barrier running up the middle of the Roman circus, forming a race track

surgeon a doctor who operates on charioteers when they are injured

trainer a person who teaches horses to race

tunic a plain shirt without buttons

waterer someone who feeds and gives water to horses

wickerwork basketwork

Index